GRAINES DE SAVOIR

Artificial intelligence for beginners: Demystify the concepts and explore the revolutionary applications of AI

Contents

1

Introduction to artificial intelligence

1.1. Definition and objectives of AI

Artificial intelligence, often abbreviated to AI, is a branch of computer science that focuses on the development of machines and systems capable of performing tasks that generally require human intelligence. These tasks include, among others, problem-solving, learning, language comprehension, visual and auditory perception, and decision-making.

One of the fundamental aims of artificial intelligence is to create machines that can think, learn and adapt autonomously. AI researchers also aim to design systems that can outperform humans in a variety of skills, including computational abilities, analyzing complex data and performing specific tasks.

In this quest, scientists and engineers are working on algorithms and models capable of processing information, identifying patterns and drawing conclusions in a similar way to the human mind. The idea is to reproduce, as far as possible, the cognitive processes that characterize our intelligence and apply them to machines and computer systems.

It's important to note that AI is not a monolithic concept, but rather a constantly evolving set of techniques, approaches and technologies. As such, artificial intelligence encompasses diverse fields, such as machine learning, robotics, computer vision, natural language processing, process automation and many others.

1.2 History and evolution of AI

The origins of artificial intelligence can be traced back to antiquity, when the first ideas of machines imitating human intelligence were conceived. However, it was in the middle of the 20th century that the concept of AI was truly born and began to develop as a scientific discipline.

In the 1950s, researchers such as Alan Turing, John McCarthy, Marvin Minsky and others laid the foundations of AI by creating theoretical models and proposing methods for solving complex problems using machines. This early work led to the emergence of symbolic AI, where systems were based on rules and symbols to represent knowledge.

In the 1980s, the focus shifted to machine learning, which

enables machines to learn from data and experience without being explicitly programmed. This approach led to the creation of numerous learning algorithms and paved the way for the emergence of deep learning in the early 21st century.

Deep learning, based on artificial neural networks, revolution-ized AI by enabling machines to process and analyze massive amounts of data in a similar way to the human brain. These ad-vances have led to significant progress in fields such as computer vision, natural language processing and speech recognition.

Over the years, artificial intelligence has also been influenced by other disciplines, such as psychology, neuroscience, philos-ophy and linguistics, which have helped shape AI theories and techniques.

Today, AI is a fast-growing and constantly evolving field, with rapid technological advances and applications in almost every aspect of our daily lives. Researchers and engineers continue to explore new ways of creating intelligent machines, building on the discoveries and innovations of the past and paving the way for an exciting future for artificial intelligence.

1.3 Artificial intelligence vs. human intelligence

Artificial intelligence and human intelligence share certain similarities, but also present some notable differences. While AI seeks to reproduce the cognitive processes of humans, machines and computer systems have distinct capabilities and limitations in relation to our own intelligence.

Human intelligence is characterized by the ability to think, reason, solve problems, understand and produce language, as well as perceive and interact with our environment. It is also marked by our awareness of ourselves and others, our creativity, our intuition and our capacity to experience emotions.

Artificial intelligence, on the other hand, is based on algorithms and mathematical models that enable machines to learn and adapt. Although AI systems can process information in a similar way to the human mind, they have no self-awareness, intuition or emotions.

One of the main differences between AI and human intelligence lies in information processing capabilities. Machines can process and analyze massive volumes of data at a speed and with a precision that humans cannot match. This capability enables AI systems to outperform humans in specific tasks, such as image recognition, language translation and complex data analysis.

However, human intelligence is more flexible and adaptable, capable of dealing with unexpected situations and solving problems that require contextual understanding and intuition. Machines, while capable of learning and adapting, are generally designed for specific tasks and may struggle to handle situations outside their domain of competence.

Ultimately, artificial intelligence and human intelligence are complementary. Machines can help us perform complex, repetitive tasks, while humans bring the creativity, intuition and contextual understanding that are often needed to solve new and novel problems.

2

Fundamental concepts of AI

2.1. Algorithms and data

Algorithms and data are essential elements of artificial intelligence, enabling machines to learn, adapt and make decisions. In this chapter, we will examine the respective roles of algorithms and data in the development of effective AI systems.

An algorithm is a series of step-by-step instructions for performing a task or solving a problem. In AI, algorithms are designed to process information, detect patterns and make decisions based on the data provided. There are many types of algorithm used in artificial intelligence, including machine learning algorithms, artificial neural networks and search and optimization algorithms.

Data is another crucial component of AI, as it feeds the algorithms and enables the machines to learn and improve. Data can be structured (e.g. tables of numbers) or unstructured (e.g. text, images or videos), and comes from a variety of sources, such as sensors, databases or online interactions.

Machine learning, an important branch of AI, relies heavily on data to train models and improve their performance. Machine learning algorithms use training data sets to adapt their parameters and generate models capable of making predictions or decisions. The greater the quantity and quality of the data, the more accurately the algorithms can learn and adapt.

2.2. Supervised, unsupervised and reinforcement learning

Machine learning is a key method in the development of artificial intelligence, enabling machines to improve and adapt to the data they process. There are three main approaches to machine learning: supervised learning, unsupervised learning and reinforcement learning. In this chapter, we will examine each of these approaches in detail.

· Supervised learning

Supervised learning is the most common form of machine learning. In this approach, algorithms are trained using a set of labeled training data, which contain both inputs (features) and the corresponding outputs (labels). The aim of supervised learning is to develop a model capable of predicting the output for new inputs based on the training examples.

Supervised learning is widely used to solve classification (categorizing data according to their labels) and regression (predicting a continuous value) problems. Examples of supervised learning algorithms include linear regression, decision trees and artificial neural networks.

· Unsupervised learning

Unlike supervised learning, unsupervised learning does not require labels for training data. Unsupervised learning algorithms attempt to discover hidden structures, patterns or relationships in the data without knowing the expected results. This approach is particularly useful for analyzing large, complex data where labels are unavailable or difficult to obtain.

The main tasks of unsupervised learning include clustering (grouping similar data) and dimensionality reduction (simplifying data while preserving its essential characteristics). Commonly used unsupervised learning algorithms include k-means partitioning, principal component analysis (PCA) and auto-encoders.

· Reinforcement learning

Reinforcement learning is a machine learning approach in which an agent learns to make decisions by interacting with its environment. Unlike supervised and unsupervised approaches, reinforcement learning focuses on finding an optimal policy for selecting actions to maximize a cumulative reward.

In reinforcement learning, the agent receives rewards or punishments depending on the quality of its actions, enabling it to progressively adjust its policy to improve its performance. Examples of reinforcement learning applications include robotics, control systems and games.

2.3 Neural networks and deep learning

Artificial neural networks and deep learning are key concepts in the field of artificial intelligence, particularly as regards machine learning. In this chapter, we explore the basics of neural networks and how deep learning takes advantage of their architecture to solve complex problems.

· Artificial neural networks

Artificial neural networks (ANNs) are computer models inspired by the functioning of the human brain and its biological neurons. An ANN is made up of computing units called artificial neurons, which are organized in successive layers. The neurons in one layer are connected to those in previous and subsequent layers, enabling information to be transmitted and calculations to be carried out.

ANNs are capable of learning from data by adjusting the weights of connections between neurons. This learning process is usually carried out using an optimization algorithm, such as gradient backpropagation, which minimizes a cost function describing the difference between the network's predictions and the expected results.

- Deep learning

Deep learning is a sub-discipline of machine learning that focuses on neural networks with many hidden layers, known as deep neural networks. These networks are capable of modeling complex, hierarchical data representations, making them particularly effective for tackling challenging problems such as image recognition, natural language understanding and speech synthesis.

Deep learning takes advantage of increasing computing power and the availability of large quantities of data to train high-performance models. Deep neural networks are often trained on graphics processing units (GPUs) or specialized hardware gas pedals to speed up the learning process.

Commonly used deep learning architectures include convolutional neural networks (CNNs), which are particularly suited to image recognition, and recurrent neural networks (RNNs), which are effective for processing sequences of data, such as time series or natural language sentences.

In short, artificial neural networks and deep learning are key concepts in artificial intelligence, enabling machines to learn and model complex representations of data. Deep learning, in particular, has led to major advances in various fields of application, thanks to its ability to handle difficult problems with deep neural network architectures.

3

AI techniques and approaches

3.1 Natural language processing (NLP)

Natural Language Processing (NLP) is a branch of artificial intelligence that focuses on the understanding, interpretation and generation of human language by machines. NLP aims to enable smooth and natural communication between humans and computers, using algorithms to analyze, process and generate text or speech. In this chapter, we look at the key concepts and applications of NLP.

Key concepts of NLP

NLP is based on several key concepts, including :

- Tokenization: breaking down text into words, phrases or

other meaningful units (called tokens) to facilitate analysis.

- Morphological analysis: study of word structure to identify grammatical forms and roots (e.g. verb conjugation and noun declension).
- Syntactic analysis: examining the grammatical structure of sentences to determine the relationships between words and word groups (such as subjects, objects and complements).
- Semantic analysis: extracting meaning from words, phrases and texts, taking into account context and real-world knowledge.
- Text generation: producing coherent, natural texts from structured or unstructured information.

NLP applications

NLP is used in a wide variety of applications, including :

- Intelligent voice assistants: Siri, Google Assistant and Alexa are examples of NLP applications that help users perform tasks by understanding and responding to voice commands.
- Machine translation: services such as Google Translate and DeepL use NLP to translate texts between different languages in real time.
- Sentiment analysis: companies use NLP to analyze customer comments, tweets and online reviews to detect positive or negative opinions about their products and services.
- Text classification: NLP algorithms can be used to automatically categorize documents, e-mails and articles according to content or subject.

- Chatbots: chatbots use NLP to understand user queries and provide appropriate responses, enhancing interaction between humans and machines.

3.2. Computer vision

Computer vision is a branch of artificial intelligence that aims to enable machines to understand and interpret images and videos in the same way as humans do. This discipline seeks to extract information from visual data and recognize objects, people, scenes and actions. In this chapter, we look at the key concepts and applications of computer vision.

Key concepts of computer vision

Computer vision is based on several key concepts, including :

- Object detection: identifying and locating specific objects in an image or video.
- Object recognition: classifying objects in an image or video according to their category or type (e.g. car, cat, dog, etc.).
- Image segmentation: dividing an image into different regions, generally based on criteria such as color, texture or contours.
- Face recognition: identification and verification of human faces in an image or video.
- Scene recognition: analysis of an image or video to un-

derstand and describe the overall scene, including objects, actions and contexts.

Computer vision applications

Computer vision is used in a multitude of applications, such as :

- Surveillance and security: video surveillance systems use computer vision to detect and track the movements of people and vehicles, and to recognize suspicious behavior or faces.
- Industrial automation: computer vision is used to inspect and control product quality, as well as to guide robots and automated machines.
- Autonomous driving: autonomous vehicles use computer vision to detect obstacles, pedestrians, road signs and other important elements in the road environment.
- Augmented reality: augmented reality applications use computer vision to superimpose digital information on real-world images captured by cameras.
- Social networks: computer vision is used to detect and recognize faces, objects and scenes in photos and videos shared on social media platforms.

3.3. Expert systems and rule-based reasoning

Expert systems are an approach to artificial intelligence that relies on sets of logical rules to simulate human reasoning and solve specific problems. They are designed to mimic the expertise of a human specialist in a particular field, and are often used for tasks requiring specialized knowledge.

Unlike other AI approaches, such as machine learning, expert systems rely on a set of explicit, deterministic rules to make decisions. These rules are usually encoded in formal language and are derived from human expertise or domain knowledge.

Rule-based reasoning is a key technique used in expert systems. It involves applying logical rules to draw conclusions from a set of facts or hypotheses. This type of reasoning enables expert systems to solve problems by following a deductive process and using explicit knowledge.

Expert systems have been widely used in fields such as medicine, finance, engineering and law. They were particularly popular in the 1980s and 1990s, before machine learning-based approaches took over. Nevertheless, expert systems remain useful in certain specific applications where explanation of decisions and transparency are crucial.

Applications of expert systems include:

- Medical diagnosis: expert systems can help doctors make diagnoses by analyzing patients' symptoms and using codified medical knowledge.

- Investment management: expert systems can help investors make investment decisions by analyzing financial data and applying rules based on the expertise of financial analysts.
- Legal advice: expert systems can help lawyers and clients solve legal problems by applying rules based on legislation and case law.
- Planning and optimization: expert systems can be used to solve complex planning and optimization problems in areas such as logistics, production and project management.

3.4. Search and planning

Search and planning are key areas of artificial intelligence that concern the way intelligent systems identify and explore solutions to achieve specific goals. These techniques enable AI systems to make informed decisions based on available information and the constraints of the problem to be solved. Here are a few approaches and applications of search and planning in AI:

Heuristic search: Heuristic search is a method for quickly finding solutions to complex problems, using rules of thumb or "heuristics" to guide the search. Heuristics are simplifying strategies that reduce the search space by eliminating unpromising options. Heuristic search algorithms, such as the A* algorithm, are commonly used to solve navigation, routing and planning problems.

Local search and optimization: Local search is a method that explores the solution space by examining neighboring alternatives to an initial solution and making incremental adjustments. Optimization algorithms, such as simulated annealing and the gradient algorithm, are examples of local search that can be used to solve complex optimization problems, such as communication network design, production planning and resource management.

Automatic planning: Automatic planning is a branch of AI that aims to generate sequences of actions to achieve specific goals, given constraints and available resources. Planning algorithms, such as the STRIPS planner and the PDDL planner, are used to solve planning problems in fields such as robotics, aerospace and logistics.

Decision support systems: Decision support systems are AI applications that provide recommendations and advice to help human decision-makers solve complex problems. These systems can use search and planning techniques to evaluate alternatives and optimize decisions according to objectives, constraints and uncertainties.

Overall, search and planning are key areas of artificial intelligence that enable intelligent systems to solve complex problems and make informed decisions. Search and planning techniques are widely used in various AI applications, ranging from navigation and optimization to automatic planning and decision support systems.

4

Practical applications of AI

4.1 AI in industry and production

Artificial intelligence has revolutionized industry and production by automating processes, improving quality and increasing efficiency. AI applications in this field are varied, touching on many aspects of the production chain, from product design to logistics and maintenance. Here are some of the most common applications of AI in industry and production:

- Process automation: AI can be used to automate complex or repetitive processes in factories, using intelligent robots and control systems. Robots can perform tasks such as assembly, welding, painting and packaging, while intelligent control systems can optimize production processes in real time.
- Quality control: AI can improve product quality by detecting

and preventing manufacturing defects. Computer vision systems can inspect products in real time and identify anomalies, while machine learning algorithms can analyze production data to detect trends and potential problems.

- Predictive maintenance: AI can be used to monitor the condition of production machines and equipment, predicting breakdowns and proactively scheduling maintenance. Machine learning algorithms can analyze sensor data and maintenance histories to determine when a machine is likely to break down, helping to avoid costly production stoppages.
- Computer-aided design (CAD): AI can help engineers design new products using optimization and simulation techniques. Genetic algorithms, reinforcement learning and neural networks can be used to generate and evaluate alternative designs, taking into account technical, economic and environmental constraints.
- Logistics and supply chain: AI can optimize logistics and the supply chain by predicting demand, planning inventories and coordinating deliveries. AI systems can analyze historical data and market trends to forecast future requirements for materials and finished products, and adjust orders and stock levels accordingly.

4.2 AI in medicine and healthcare

Artificial intelligence is having a significant impact on the field of medicine and healthcare, improving diagnoses, personalizing treatments and optimizing patient care.

Here are just a few applications of AI in medicine and healthcare:

- Medical diagnostics: AI algorithms, particularly those based on deep learning, are used to analyze medical images, such as X-rays, MRIs and CT scans, to detect abnormalities or signs of disease. These systems can help doctors make more accurate and rapid diagnoses, reducing medical errors and improving outcomes for patients.

- Personalized medicine: AI can help personalize medical treatments by analyzing patients' genetic, environmental and behavioral data to determine the most suitable therapies. AI systems can also predict a patient's response to a drug or treatment, enabling doctors to choose the best option for each individual.

- Surgical assistance: AI-assisted robots are increasingly being used to perform complex surgical procedures, providing superior precision and control. These robots can help reduce complications, infections and recovery times, while improving patient outcomes.

- Medical records management: AI can facilitate medical records management by automating data entry, identifying errors and facilitating access to information. Natural language processing systems can be used to analyze and interpret textual data, such as clinical notes and medical reports.

· Telemedicine: AI systems can support telemedicine by providing virtual consultations, analyzing patient data remotely and monitoring their state of health. This can help improve access to medical care, particularly for patients living in rural or remote areas.

· Medical research: AI can accelerate medical research by analyzing large datasets to identify new therapeutic targets, designing drugs and evaluating their effectiveness. AI systems can also help plan and analyze clinical trial results, identifying factors that influence outcomes and optimizing study protocols.

The applications of AI in medicine and healthcare are diverse, offering significant benefits in terms of diagnosis, treatment and patient care management. By harnessing the power of AI, healthcare professionals can deliver more accurate, personalized and effective care, while improving patient outcomes.

· Prevention and public health: AI can help monitor and

predict epidemics and public health problems, by analyzing epidemiological, environmental and socio-economic data. AI systems can also help promote disease prevention by identifying risk factors, supporting screening programs and guiding public health interventions.

- Care management: AI can help optimize the coordination and management of patient care, supporting clinical decision-making, planning treatments and monitoring medication adherence. AI systems can also help identify patients' healthcare service needs and allocate resources more efficiently.

- Medical training and education: AI can support the training and education of healthcare professionals by providing simulation, assessment and feedback tools to improve their clinical skills. AI systems can also facilitate access to medical knowledge, helping healthcare professionals stay abreast of the latest advances in research, diagnosis and treatment.

In short, artificial intelligence is revolutionizing the field of medicine and healthcare, offering opportunities for improved diagnosis, treatment and management of patient care. The applications of AI in medicine and healthcare are numerous and will continue to develop as the technology advances, helping to improve the quality and efficiency of medical care.

4.3 AI in finance and commerce

Artificial intelligence is increasingly used in the financial and commercial sector to improve processes, reduce costs and increase efficiency.

Here are just a few applications of AI in finance and commerce:

- Market analysis: AI systems can analyze large datasets from a variety of sources, such as financial news, economic data and social media, to anticipate market trends and price fluctuations. This analysis can help investors and traders make informed decisions and optimize their investment strategies.

- Algorithmic trading: AI is increasingly used to create automated trading algorithms, which can analyze market data in real time, identify investment opportunities and place orders quickly and efficiently. AI-assisted trading algorithms can react more quickly to market changes, reducing risk and increasing profits.

- Portfolio management: AI systems can help manage investment portfolios by analyzing data on assets, risks and returns, and generating recommendations for optimizing asset allocation. AI can also be used to continuously monitor portfolio performance and adjust positions according to market conditions and investor objectives.

- Fraud detection: AI can help detect and prevent financial fraud by analyzing transactions and customer behavior to identify suspicious or abnormal activity. Fraud detection algorithms can learn to recognize patterns of fraudulent behavior and quickly report incidents to financial institutions.

- Digital banking and financial services: AI systems are increasingly being used to enhance the customer experience in digital banking and financial services. Chatbots and virtual assistants can provide personalized information and support, while data analytics algorithms can help tailor financial products and services to individual customer needs.

- Risk management: AI can help financial institutions assess and manage risk by analyzing data on customers, markets and financial products. AI systems can also help anticipate and mitigate the impact of economic, political and environmental events on financial markets.

- Credit and risk assessment: AI systems can assess customers' credit risk by analyzing various data, such as credit history, income, expenses and payment behavior. Credit risk assessment algorithms can help financial institutions make more accurate lending decisions and reduce losses due to defaults.

Artificial intelligence is transforming the finance and commerce sector by automating and optimizing many processes. The applications of AI in this field are diverse and continue to develop as the technology evolves. By harnessing the power of AI, financial institutions and commercial enterprises can improve performance, reduce costs and deliver a more personalized and efficient customer experience.

4.4 AI in education and training

Artificial intelligence has the potential to transform education and training by making learning more personalized, efficient and accessible.

Here are some applications of AI in education and training:

- Adaptive learning: AI systems can analyze learners' performance and preferences to create personalized learning paths. By adapting the content and pace of learning to individual needs, AI can help students progress faster and understand concepts better.

- Intelligent tutoring: AI-assisted virtual tutors and learning assistants can provide personalized pedagogical support, answer students' questions and give advice to improve skills and knowledge. Intelligent tutors can help bridge the gaps in traditional education by offering individualized support to each student.

- Automated assessment: AI systems can automate the assessment of student work, marking exams, assignments and projects quickly and accurately. Assessment algorithms can also provide detailed, constructive feedback to help students identify their strengths and weaknesses.

- Open educational resources: AI can facilitate access to online educational resources, recommending relevant content and tailoring resources to learners' needs. AI systems can also help organize and structure educational resources to facilitate search and navigation.

- Vocational training: AI systems can help workers acquire new skills and train for new jobs, by recommending customized training programs and providing pedagogical support. AI can also be used to assess workers' skills and identify areas for improvement.

· Recommender systems: AI systems can help students and educators discover new educational resources, by recommending courses, articles, books and tools based on their interests and needs. Recommender systems can also help identify resources that are most relevant and effective for learning.

· Virtual reality and augmented reality: AI can be used to create immersive and interactive learning environments, using virtual reality (VR) and augmented reality (AR) to simulate real-life situations and provide hands-on learning experiences.

4.5. AI in entertainment and video games

Artificial intelligence is also having a significant impact on entertainment and video games, enhancing the user experience and creating more realistic and immersive virtual worlds.

Here are just a few AI applications in this field:

- Non-player characters (NPCs): AI makes it possible to create more realistic and interactive NPCs in video games. AI-assisted NPCs can make more complex decisions, display more human-like behaviors and react dynamically to player actions, enhancing the gaming experience.

- Procedural Content Generation (PCG): AI can be used to automatically generate game elements such as levels, objects or environments. This technique, known as procedural content generation, makes it possible to create vast and varied virtual worlds without the need to manually create each individual element.

- Scenario building: AI systems can help build more complex, interactive game scenarios by adapting the game's story and events to the player's actions. This helps create more personalized and captivating gaming experiences.

- Machine learning for game design: Game developers can use AI to analyze player play data and identify trends, preferences and potential problems. This information can be used to optimize and improve game design, based on players' needs and expectations.

- Strategy and chess games: AI has revolutionized strategy and chess games, creating virtual opponents capable of competing with the best human players. AI programs such as AlphaGo and Stockfish use deep learning and exploration algorithms to analyze millions of possible positions and strategies, enabling them to make optimal decisions during the game.

- Virtual reality and augmented reality: AI is also being used to enhance virtual reality (VR) and augmented reality (AR) experiences by creating immersive, interactive environments. AI systems can generate objects and scenes in real time, based on users' actions and movements, to deliver a more realistic and engaging gaming experience.

- Speech recognition and interaction: AI can be used to enhance interaction between players and video games using speech recognition and natural language processing. This enables players to give voice commands, ask questions and interact with NPCs in a more natural and intuitive way.

5

Ethical and societal challenges of AI

5.1. Bias and discrimination

Artificial intelligence raises important ethical and societal issues, particularly with regard to bias and discrimination. AI systems rely on data sets to learn and make decisions. However, this data may contain unintended biases or pre-existing stereotypes, which can lead to discrimination in AI results or recommendations.

Data provenance:
The datasets used to train AI algorithms are often drawn from the real world and may reflect existing inequalities and biases in society. If the data is biased, AI systems can reproduce and amplify these biases when making decisions or performing tasks.

Lack of diversity:

A lack of diversity among AI designers and developers can contribute to the unintentional introduction of bias and discrimination. Diverse development teams are more likely to identify and address issues of bias and discrimination in AI systems.

Transparency and explainability:

The complexity of AI algorithms and the opacity of some deep learning models make it difficult to understand decision-making processes. This can lead to problems of accountability and trust, particularly when AI systems produce discriminatory or unfair results.

Regulation and legislation:

Governments and international organizations are beginning to recognize the ethical and societal issues associated with AI and are putting regulations in place to minimize bias and discrimination. These regulations aim to ensure that AI systems are fair, transparent and respectful of human rights.

Awareness-raising and education:

To combat bias and discrimination in AI, it is essential to raise awareness of ethical and societal issues among AI designers, developers and users. AI education and training programs should include modules on ethics, bias and social responsibility.

Debiasing techniques:

Researchers are developing techniques to identify and correct biases in AI datasets and algorithms. These techniques include resampling, modifying training data and using fairness metrics to evaluate the performance of AI systems.

In summary, bias and discrimination are major ethical and societal issues in the field of artificial intelligence. Recognizing and addressing these issues is crucial to ensuring that AI systems are fair, equitable and beneficial to all.

5.2. Data confidentiality and security

Data confidentiality and security are crucial issues in the field of artificial intelligence, as AI systems often handle large amounts of sensitive and personal data.

Here are some points to consider to ensure data protection and security for AI systems:

Data collection and storage: Companies and organizations that develop and use AI systems must implement robust security measures to protect the data collected and stored. This includes using encryption methods, securing servers and authenticating data access.

Consent and transparency: Users must be informed of how their data is collected, processed and used by AI systems. Companies must obtain users' consent before collecting their data, and be transparent about how data is used to make decisions.

Anonymization and data protection: Anonymization and data protection techniques, such as pseudonymization, can be used to preserve the confidentiality of data processed by AI systems. These techniques make it difficult to identify individuals from the data, while enabling AI algorithms to learn and make decisions.

Accountability and governance: Companies and organizations need to put in place governance and accountability mechanisms to ensure the data protection and security of AI systems. This may include appointing a Data Protection Officer (DPO) and putting in place policies and procedures to monitor and control data use.

Regulation and legislation: Governments and international organizations are adopting regulations to protect data privacy and security in the context of artificial intelligence. The European Union's General Data Protection Regulation (GDPR) is an example of regulation aimed at protecting personal data and ensuring transparency and accountability in data processing.

Cyberattacks and AI system security: AI systems can be vulnerable to cyberattacks, such as data theft, algorithm hijacking and data injection attacks. Companies and organizations need to implement security measures to protect their AI systems against these threats.

Federated learning and privacy: Federated learning is a technique that enables AI algorithms to learn from decentralized data without having to collect and store all the data in one place. This can improve data confidentiality and security by reducing the risk of leakage or unauthorized access.

5.3 Impact on jobs and skills

Artificial intelligence is having a significant impact on the labor market and the skills required for the jobs of tomorrow.

Here are some key points concerning the effects of AI on employment and skills:

Task automation: AI systems are capable of automating many repetitive and routine tasks, which can increase productivity and efficiency in various sectors. However, this can also lead to the elimination of certain jobs, particularly those that are heavily focused on manual, repetitive tasks.

Creating new jobs: while AI may automate certain tasks, it also creates new jobs and opportunities in areas such as software development, AI research, AI-related project management and data analysis. Workers may need to retrain or acquire new skills to take advantage of these opportunities.

Evolving skills requirements: As the adoption of AI grows, the skills sought by employers are also evolving. Workers will need to develop complex problem-solving, critical thinking, communication and collaboration skills to succeed in an increasingly automated work environment.

Training and education: education systems will need to adapt to prepare students for the challenges posed by AI and help them develop the skills required to succeed in the job market. This may include the introduction of curricula focused on AI skills, e-learning and lifelong learning.

Economic and social inequalities: the impact of AI on employment may exacerbate economic and social inequalities if certain categories of workers are more affected by automation than others. Governments and organizations will need to put policies in place to support workers affected by changes in the labor market and encourage equal opportunities.

Decent work and working conditions: The integration of AI into the workplace may also raise questions about working conditions and workers' rights. Employers and governments will need to ensure that the adoption of AI is carried out ethically and responsibly, respecting decent work standards and protecting workers' rights.

5.4. Responsibility and decision-making

Artificial intelligence raises important questions about responsibility and decision-making, particularly when AI systems are used to make decisions that have an impact on individuals and society.

Here are some key points to consider on this subject:

Transparency and explicability: AI systems should be designed to be transparent and explicable, so that users and stakeholders can understand how decisions are made and on what basis. This is essential to ensure accountability and trust in AI systems.

Human accountability: Although AI systems can make autonomous decisions, it is important to maintain human accountability for the actions and decisions taken by these systems. Organizations and individuals who deploy and use AI systems must be held accountable for the consequences of their decisions, whether positive or negative.

Ethics and values: AI systems should be designed and developed to respect ethical principles and human values. This may include ensuring that AI systems do not discriminate, respect privacy and data confidentiality, and make fair and balanced decisions.

Legislation and regulation: Governments and international organizations will need to adopt laws and regulations to frame responsibility and decision-making in the context of artificial intelligence. These regulations should ensure that AI systems are used ethically and responsibly, and that they conform to societal norms and values.

Audits and controls: AI systems should be subject to regular audits and controls to ensure that they operate ethically and responsibly. This may include external checks on regulatory compliance, performance testing and social impact assessments.

Stakeholder participation: Decision-making regarding the development and use of AI systems should involve a wide range of stakeholders, including users, ethics experts, civil society representatives and policymakers. This will ensure that decisions taken reflect the needs and concerns of all parties concerned.

In conclusion, accountability and decision-making are key issues in the field of artificial intelligence. Companies, governments and society as a whole will need to work together to ensure that AI systems are used ethically and responsibly, and that they respect society's fundamental values and principles.

6

The future of artificial intelligence

6.1. Innovations and emerging trends

Artificial intelligence (AI) continues to develop rapidly, with new innovations and trends that could transform many industries in the years to come.

Here are some of the most promising trends to watch:

Explainable AI: Explainable AI focuses on the transparency and explainability of decisions made by AI systems. AI systems are increasingly used in areas such as finance, healthcare and justice, where fair and transparent decisions are crucial. It is therefore important to understand how AI systems make decisions and to be able to explain these decisions in an understandable way.

Ethical AI: Ethical AI is an approach that aims to ensure that AI systems are developed and used responsibly and ethically, taking into account social and ethical considerations. Ethical issues related to AI, such as bias and discrimination, are increasingly discussed and require an ethical approach to ensure responsible use of the technology.

Conversational AI: It allows users to communicate with AI systems in a natural and intuitive way, using voice or text. This technology is increasingly used for virtual assistants, chatbots and user interfaces. Conversational AI applications can include automated customer service systems, virtual personal assistants for the home or office, or real-time translation applications.

Autonomous AI: It refers to AI systems that can make decisions and act autonomously, without human intervention. This technology is used in areas such as autonomous driving and autonomous robots. Autonomous AI applications can include delivery drones, autonomous vehicles, or manufacturing or assembly robots.

AI in the cloud: AI in the cloud allows users to have AI capabilities on demand, without having to invest in expensive infrastructure. This technology is increasingly used for natural language processing, computer vision and data analysis applications. AI applications in the cloud can include data analysis tools, speech recognition systems, or security and surveillance applications.

AI in health: AI is increasingly used in the field of health, for the early detection of diseases, the analysis of medical data and the personalization of treatments. This technology has the potential to revolutionize personalized medicine, enabling more precise treatments tailored to individual patient needs.

AI in energy: AI is also increasingly used in the energy sector, for the optimization of energy production and the management of smart energy networks. Applications of AI in energy can include renewable energy production forecasting systems, energy consumption management systems, or energy quality monitoring systems.

It is important to note that these trends are not mutually exclusive, and many AI systems incorporate several of these technologies and approaches. Moreover, these emerging trends also raise important ethical and social issues, which require proper thought and regulation to ensure responsible use of technology.

6.2. Regulation and governance of AI

The regulation and governance of AI are important topics, given growing concerns about the ethical risks and social impacts of the technology. Governments and organizations are working to put in place regulatory frameworks to govern the use of AI in different sectors.

Several countries have already established AI regulatory and governance plans. The European Union, for example, published an action plan on AI in 2018, which offers guidelines for the responsible use of technology. In 2021, the European Union also published draft AI regulations, which aim to regulate the use of

AI in the EU and build trust in the technology.

In the United States, the White House released a national strategy for AI in 2019, which emphasizes innovation, security and privacy. In 2020, the US Congress also created the National Commission on AI, tasked with advising the US government on the use of AI.

Internationally, the Organization for Economic Co-operation and Development (OECD) released AI Guidelines in 2019, which aim to promote responsible and ethical use of technology around the world.

In addition to these regulatory frameworks, it is also important to put in place governance mechanisms to monitor the use of AI and address ethical and social issues that may arise. Organizations can work with ethics and technology experts to develop guidelines for the use of AI, or create oversight committees to monitor technology use and take action when problems arise.

6.3. Collaboration between humans and AI

Collaboration between humans and AI systems is increasingly common in many industries, and is likely to become even more prevalent in the future. This collaboration can take many forms, ranging from complementarity between human skills and AI capabilities to direct collaboration between humans and AI systems.

In some cases, AI can be used to enhance human capabilities, helping to process big data, make more informed decisions, or automate repetitive, routine tasks. For example, AI is often used in finance and accounting to perform data processing tasks that would be tedious or difficult for humans to perform manually.

In other cases, AI can be used to work directly with humans, using human-machine interfaces to enable closer collaboration. For example, AI can be used to help doctors diagnose diseases by analyzing medical data, or to help lawyers prepare legal documents using natural language processing algorithms.

However, the collaboration between humans and AI systems also raises important ethical and social questions, especially regarding the responsibilities and consequences of decisions made by AI systems. It is therefore important to put in place governance mechanisms to monitor and regulate the use of AI in these collaborative contexts.

Ultimately, collaboration between humans and AI systems can provide many opportunities to improve human performance and capabilities in many areas. However, it is important to ensure that this collaboration is done in a responsible and ethical manner, taking into account the potential social and ethical consequences of using technology.

6.4. Challenges and opportunities for society

AI offers tremendous opportunities to improve many aspects of human life, but it also raises significant challenges for society as a whole.

Here are some of the most significant challenges and opportunities:

Jobs and skills: AI is likely to radically change the labor market, with potential impacts on jobs, skills and wages. Companies will need to anticipate these changes and prepare workers for the new skills and tasks that will emerge.

Education and training: Educators and trainers must also prepare for potential changes related to AI, adapting education and training programs to prepare students for new skills and new labor market demands.

Inequalities and biases: AI has the potential to reinforce social inequalities and biases, depending on the quality of data used to train AI systems. Developers and policymakers must therefore work to ensure that AI systems are developed responsibly and ethically, to avoid unfair or discriminatory consequences.

Privacy and security: AI systems can potentially collect and use personal data in invasive ways, which raises privacy and security issues. Policymakers must work to ensure that users have control over their own data and that AI systems are protected against security threats.

Ethics and Accountability: AI raises important ethical questions, especially regarding accountability and decision-making. Policymakers must work to ensure that AI systems are developed and used responsibly and ethically, taking into account the potential impacts on society as a whole.

In sum, AI offers tremendous opportunities to improve human life in many areas, but it also raises significant challenges for society as a whole. It is therefore important that policy makers work to anticipate these challenges and develop strategies to deal with the potential social and ethical consequences of the technology.

7

Real-world applications of AI

7.1. Chatbots and virtual agents

Chatbots and virtual agents are computer programs that use AI to communicate with users in natural language, simulating a human conversation. They are used in a wide range of fields, such as customer service, e-commerce, healthcare and financial services.

Chatbots can be programmed to answer common customer questions, to perform simple tasks like booking appointments, or to provide information about products or services. Virtual agents, on the other hand, are digital avatars that can interact with users in virtual environments, such as video games or training simulations.

The benefits of chatbots and virtual agents are numerous. They can be used 24 hours a day, 7 days a week, allowing a quick response to customer requests. They are also able to handle multiple conversations simultaneously, which improves operational efficiency. In addition, their use can reduce personnel costs and improve customer satisfaction.

However, there are also challenges when using chatbots and virtual agents. They must be programmed with a thorough understanding of the domain for which they are used, in order to respond precisely to customer demands. Additionally, they should be designed to provide a friendly and engaging user experience, otherwise customers may feel frustrated or dissatisfied.

Ultimately, chatbots and virtual agents are an example of the successful use of AI in the real world. Their use can improve operational efficiency, customer satisfaction, and business profitability.

7.2. Facial recognition and biometrics

Facial recognition is an AI technology that uses algorithms to identify and verify a person's identity based on their facial characteristics. This technology is used in many fields, including security, financial services, advertising and marketing.

Facial recognition systems can be used for applications such as airport security, physical access control, employee attendance tracking, and fraud prevention. Law enforcement can also use this technology to identify suspected criminals or missing persons.

However, facial recognition also raises privacy and security concerns. Concerns with the use of this technology include the risk of illegal surveillance, profiling and discrimination. There are also concerns about the quality of the data used to train the algorithms, which can lead to biased and inaccurate results.

Biometrics is another area of AI that uses a person's physical characteristics for identification. Biometric techniques can include facial recognition, but also fingerprint identification, retina identification and voice recognition. These techniques are often used for employee or customer identification in the security, financial services, and healthcare industries.

As with facial recognition, the use of biometrics raises privacy and security concerns. There are also concerns about the quality of biometric data used for identification, which may be inaccurate or biased.

Overall, facial recognition and biometrics are ever-evolving technologies that offer advantages and disadvantages. It is important to consider privacy and security concerns when using these technologies and to ensure that appropriate steps are taken to protect the data and rights of the individual.

7.3. Recommender systems

Recommender systems are another example of the practical application of AI in our daily lives. These systems use machine learning algorithms to analyze data and predict user preferences or interests. Recommendations may be based on shopping habits, ratings, reviews, interactions and other data.

Recommender systems are used in a variety of areas, including:

- E-commerce: Online shopping sites use recommendation systems to recommend products that are similar or complementary to customers' previous purchases.
- Online music and video: Music and video streaming services use recommendation systems to recommend songs, artists or movies similar to those the user has already listened to or watched.
- Social media: Social media platforms use recommendation systems to recommend accounts, pages or groups to follow based on user interests.
- Advertising: Advertisers use recommendation systems to deliver targeted advertisements based on user preferences and habits.

However, the use of these systems is not without risks, as they can reinforce existing biases and stereotypes. Recommendations may be based on historical data which may not necessarily reflect current user preferences, or may be influenced by factors such as gender, race or age. It is therefore important to monitor and regulate the use of these systems to avoid discrimination.

8

Conclusion: Embrace AI and prepare for the future

T he artificial intelligence revolution is underway and it will continue to have a major impact on the world in the years to come. AI is already present in many aspects of our daily lives, from voice recognition in personal assistants and product recommendations on e-commerce sites, to detecting fraud in financial transactions and helping to making complex medical decisions.

The implementation of AI in these areas has already significantly improved the performance and efficiency of systems, as well as providing new solutions to complex problems. The potential benefits of AI are immense and extend to a wide range of fields, including medicine, education, science, industry and finance.

However, AI also raises significant challenges, especially regarding the social and ethical consequences of the technology. Biases in algorithms, collection and use of personal data, accountability for decisions made by autonomous systems, consumer and employee protection, and impacts on jobs and skills are all issues that need to be addressed. taken into account.

It is therefore essential that decision makers work to ensure that AI is developed and used in a responsible and ethical way, taking into account the potential consequences on society as a whole. It is also important that governments, businesses, universities and civil society organizations work together to ensure that the technology is accessible to everyone, and that the benefits of AI are shared equitably.

Ultimately, the future of AI is in our hands. We can choose to embrace technology and work together to reap its benefits, while solving the challenges it poses. We can also choose to sit on the sidelines and let AI develop without our active participation. However, if we choose the first option, we can shape the future of AI and prepare a better and fairer society for future generations.